GW00392568

# Tantallon Castle

by the late Dr J. S. RICHARDSON

EDINBURGH
HER MAJESTY'S STATIONERY OFFICE

*First edition* 1937
*Second edition* 1950
*Third edition* 1980

ISBN 0 11 491537 7

# DESCRIPTION

Tantallon, situated on the coast about 4 kms to the east of the Royal Burgh of North Berwick, commands from its battlements a wide prospect of land and sea from the Lammermuir to the Lomond hills. Within 3·2 kms the Bass, that 'auld crag', stands sentinel in the Firth of Forth.

Standing on a promontory, the castle is protected to seaward by cliffs rising 30·5 m high; on the landward side the approach to the castle is defended by outworks. There is an outer entrenchment some 183 m from the building but it is uncertain whether this is a defensive feature or a counter-work raised by an attacking force.

## Outworks

The main outer defence is a great dry ditch with a high inner rampart of earth and a low outer one. Within this ditch are two earthen traverses connected with a ravelin projecting westward. At the eastern end the ditch is cut through the rock and originally terminated at the cliff. At this end the inner side of the ditch has been faced with a rubble wall and it seems unlikely that this revetment was ever carried farther westward than is indicated by the existing remains of masonry. The east end of the wall terminated at the OUTER GATE by which the approach road, passing over a wooden bridge, entered the castle BAILEY. This gateway was arched, furnished with a massive double door and defended by a gun-looped spur-work consisting of a flanking wall backed by a wooden platform and terminating in a round tower two storeys high. These features and the facing of the ditch are of sixteenth-century date. Shortly after the flanking wall was built the ditch immediately in front of the gateway was deepened considerably, forming a pit, and to command this a gun-port was formed in the extended foundation. On the farther side of the burn which flanks the old roadway is a strong defensive feature in the form of a natural hollow enlarged by quarrying. Within the bailey, east of the spur-work and close to the cliff edge, two human skeletons buried east and west were located, indicating that this part has been used as a burial ground probably during a period of siege. Some distance in front of the Mid Tower stands a seventeenth-century DOVECOT containing two chambers fitted with stone nesting-places, and south of this foundations of out-house buildings of late date were uncovered. An inner great ditch extends across the promontory from cliff to cliff, immediately in front of the castle. The solum is cut through the rock and the inner side forms a glacis at the foot of the curtain walls.

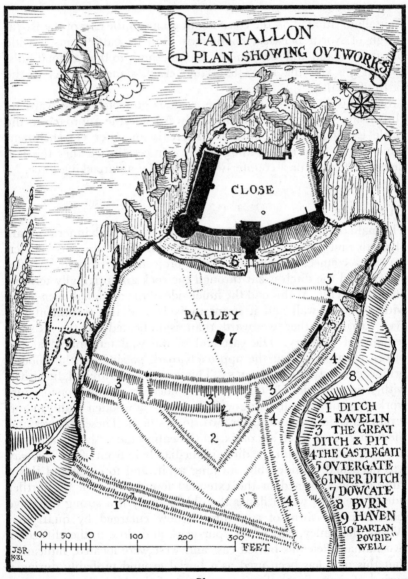

TANTALLON
PLAN SHOWING OVTWORKS

CLOSE

BAILEY

1 DITCH
2 RAVELIN
3 THE GREAT
   DITCH & PIT
4 THE CASTLEGATT
5 OVTERGATE
6 INNER DITCH
7 DOWCATE
8 BVRN
9 HAVEN
10 "PARTAN
   POVRIE"
   WELL

100  50  0      100    200    300  FEET

JSR
1931.

*Plan*

4

The castle buildings may be assigned to the latter part of the fourteenth century when Scotland began to recover after the Wars of Independence. They were subject, however, to additions and alterations in the sixteenth century. Within the courtyard and running north-east from near the north corner of the Mid Tower, the foundation of a well-built wall was uncovered. This wall, measuring 1·8 m in width and about 9·1 m in length, appeared to be older than the castle building.

On plan the castle is of the courtyard type and some of its features resemble those of the fourteenth-century chateaux of France. The builder was possibly William, the first Earl of Douglas, who was wounded at Poitiers when fighting for the French. The building, carefully planned to suit the site, consists of a gatehouse called the MID TOWER, flanked by great curtain walls 15·2 m high, which stretch across the promontory terminating at the one end in the EAST TOWER and at the other in the DOUGLAS TOWER, and of a wing on the north side of the CLOSE or courtyard which contained the Hall. A massive south curtain wall was also intended but never completed; neither was a building overlooking the cliff on the eastern side.

It is only by studying the outside of the castle that its original appearance can be appreciated. The descriptive order is as follows: the Mid Tower and Barbican, the East Tower, the Douglas Tower, and the Northern range.

## The Gatehouse or Mid Tower

Before the addition of the barbican and sixteenth-century forework [to be recognised by the greenish stone with red freestone bands], the most imposing feature of the castle front was the MID TOWER, which had a forework of twin jambs set salient to the curtain. These jambs, rising from the ditch level, were rectangular on plan till they reached the level of the floor of the second storey of the tower; above this they were corbelled out into rounds or turrets and carried up to the full height of the building. From the first floor upwards the jambs contained small chambers entered from the main apartments. The corbelling had a central machicolation on each face and the rounds were connected at the level of the third floor by a narrow bridge having a pointed arch.

The main entrance gateway is recessed. In front of it, between the jambs and over a pit, was a drawbridge worked by chains which when down was united with a permanent timber bridge set on stone supports. Above the gateway, at the second floor level, was a window [now only visible on the inside] and over this there may have been a panel bearing the Douglas coat of arms. A higher window overlooked the parapet bridge and to the south of it was a machicolated and corbelled projection connected with a chimney flue. The remains of this feature can still be seen.

The tower-head was embattled and had a low, lead-covered timber roof. At each corner, overlooking the close, there was a small round and midway between these, over the gateway, there is a machicolated projection connected with the chimney flues; part of this feature is still evident. The stair head terminated above the parapet level in a cap-house furnished with two small angle rounds.

## Barbican

Shortly after the completion of the Mid Tower the ditch was widened and a BARBICAN, of which only a fragment now remains, was built to strengthen the defence of the entrance. The castle gateway and drawbridge were then brought forward a distance of 12·2 m. The drawbridge, when lowered, rested on a pier of masonry built on the landward slope of the ditch, and, when raised, was housed in a recess flanked by engaged rounds rising from the solum. The barbican, roofed in wood, contained an entrance which was floored partly in wood; below was a pit. The latter was entered from the ditch by two round-headed doorways set opposite to each other in the lateral walls. A mural stairway in the east wall led to the flat roof of the barbican.

## Sixteenth-Century Forework

In the years following 1529 a marked alteration was effected on the front of the Mid Tower. As a result of the siege the upper part of the original forework had collapsed and it became necessary to strengthen the front of the castle against artillery attack. The entry, which permitted the passage of horse and wagon, was blocked by masonry leaving only a narrow passage, 900 mm wide, furnished with several doorways, four of which had iron yetts. A massive wall, constructed between the jambs, was built 3·5 m forward of the original forework, partially enveloping the barbican. This work, carried up to the wall-walk level, concealed the high bridge connecting the jambs. In the upper part the void between the turrets was completely packed with masonry. The much-weathered coat of arms on the forework is that of the Earl of Angus. There is no evidence to show how the wall-top of the late forework was finished in stone, but at a still later period it had a rampart of turf.

At this time the barbican was also consolidated; flat stone vaults were introduced and gun-loops inserted in the lateral walls. A roughly constructed and steep stairway, furnished at the top with a trap-door, led down from the passage to a reconstructed vault. The interior of the barbican was commanded by a gun-looped vaulted chamber in the thickness of the wall immediately over the round-headed doorway which now provides the entrance to the castle. From the doorway a narrow passage, relieved on each side by a gun-port commanding the ditch, leads to the original entrance of the Mid Tower. This gateway, of fourteenth-century date, is moulded on the outer side and has a pointed arch which springs from a moulded impost. The seating for the trunnion of the first period drawbridge and also part of the original pit can be seen. After the addition of the barbican the pit was bridged over with timber joists and decking and eventually filled up in the sixteenth century. The vertical channels for the portcullis are on either side of the entry. When drawn the portcullis was housed in a chase in the wall, immediately under the window of the apartment on the second floor.

The entry was vaulted and led through a large round-headed gate-way, which was reduced when the late forework was added to a close. At either end of the entry was a massive double door and midway there was a third door, or an iron yett. Behind the doorways can be seen the slots for large oak drawbars. On the south side of the entry was a vaulted guard room and on the north a vaulted passage admitted to a straight stairway which led to a turnpike giving access to the four storeys of the tower and the wall-head. In the sixteenth century the turnpike was built up from the first floor to the level of the curtain wall-walk and a new stair tower provided in the adjoining re-entrant angle. Each storey of the Mid Tower contained a single apartment floored with wood. Fireplaces with moulded jambs and projecting hoods can be seen in the north-east wall, but the one on the fifth floor is in the opposite wall. Garderobes and small chambers in the eastern curtain and the chambers in the jambs were entered off these apartments.

## Draw-Well

Immediately within the close is the castle DRAW-WELL, circular in shape and sunk in the rock to a depth of 32·3 m. The well was discovered at the end of last century by the late Sir Walter Hamilton Dalrymple of North Berwick and was cleared out at that time.

## East Tower

The EAST TOWER is very ruinous owing to bombardment by cannon and later quarrying operations. It originally contained five storeys floored with wood. On each floor was an apartment which was entered from the turnpike stair, but that on the ground floor was entered directly from the close. Each room had several windows, one of which faced the sea, and the others the landward side. They were furnished with stone seats. The fireplace and mural garderobe of each chamber were in the wall which extended up from the face of the cliff. In the third floor chamber is a doorway intended to give access to the wall-walk of a curtain wall which was never built. The only remaining window of this chamber has had a projecting iron grille suggesting that the room was used for the confinement of state prisoners. The upper chamber was vaulted and the platform roof of the tower had a corbelled and embattled parapet, above which rose the roof of the head of the turnpike stair. The tower-head shows evidence of patching.

In the sixteenth century the wood floors were replaced by flat stone vaults and the three lower storeys of the tower were transformed into two massive vaulted chambers, gun-looped on the landward side. This work of consolidation can be recognised by the grey-green stone, which is similar to that of the underlying cliff. Outside this masonry the curved original wall and the position of the fireplace and windows are to be seen.

## Douglas Tower

All that remains of the outline of this larger terminal tower, the DOUGLAS TOWER, is to be seen at the base and this contains the pit-prison on a level considerably below that of the courtyard. Reached by a mural stairway, it has a floor of bedrock and a long narrow shaft for ventilation. A narrow stair in the north-east angle leads to a garderobe. Above the prison were six storeys, floored with wood, each comprising a single chamber with an attached vaulted garderobe. The rooms were reached by an entrance leading from a turnpike stair. The upper chamber was vaulted and the tower-head fortified. The windows were all on the landward side and indications of these remain.

## Curtain Walls

The CURTAIN WALLS are over 3·7 m thick, and at their top an 'allerne' or wall-walk connects the towers. Each was provided with a stairway independent of those connecting the tower chambers. Off the stairways are small mural chambers with narrow window slits to the outside and small windows to the courtyard. The lower parts of these stairways have a contiguous arrangement of arches, a distinctive architectural feature of the castle. During the sixteenth century, when the castle was in Crown hands, the stairways and their mural chambers were packed with masonry and this was only removed at the close of last century. In some of the mural chambers, however, evidence of the packing has been left. All the other stairways were robbed of their steps when the castle was used as a quarry.

On the courtyard side against the east curtain was a gabled lean-to structure or 'Toofall' providing small chambers and a long loft. The roof of this lean-to was raised and an additional floor inserted in the fifteenth century. There was also a small building of a secondary nature against the west curtain.

Originally the wall-walks were enclosed within parapet walls and were roofed, the outer wall being crenellated but not corbelled; the existing corbels and embattled parapet are later alterations.

## Northern Courtyard Range

The western half of the NORTHERN RANGE is contemporary with the towers and curtain; originally it contained three storeys, floored with wood. The ground floor apartment was the 'Laigh Hall'. In the outer wall was a hooded fireplace, two long window slits and a mural garderobe. The entrance and windows were on the courtyard side, the latter being provided with stone window-seats. Over this apartment was the 'Lang Hall', so termed in a 1670 inventory. The arrangement of this chamber was similar to that in the one below except that the entrance is in the gable wall facing the Douglas Tower and was approached by a stair. The floor joists of the apartment above were housed in the walls but later this construction was altered and beams, supported on double corbels, were introduced. The upper storey, which was lighted by small arched windows on the courtyard side, was entered from a passage connected with the wall-walk on the seaward side of the building. In the sixteenth century this building was remodelled and connected with the stairway in the Douglas Tower. The ground floor was converted into three vaulted cellars and a vaulted alley running the length of the building with doorways at either end. The 'Lang Hall', which then had a tiled floor, was heightened and the upper storey was reduced to a loft and the doorway widened. The windows with one exception were enlarged, the double corbels removed and the existing large corbels introduced at a higher level. The west gable wall shows a recessed feature by which the construction of the original timber roof is made clear. This roof would appear to have been protected with lead while the later roof was slated with slates from Angus. Over the entrance are indications of there having been a gallery and screen.

When the alterations were made in the HALL building the eastern half of the range was built to the same height. This addition is now very ruinous. The ground floor was divided into three vaulted compartments, entered from the close. They include a KITCHEN and a BAKEHOUSE. The former has two fireplaces, one of which contains a small oven and slop. The bakehouse has been provided with two ovens, contained within a small building, projecting cliffwards. The larger oven was lined with marine stone from North Berwick and the throat of the other retains fragments of tile lining. The two upper floors may have contained the 'dyneing roume', 'the chamber caled my ladie's chamber', as indicated by the 1670 inventory, and other private apartments. These were entered from a turnpike stair on the courtyard side, the foundations of which can be seen. This building has been greatly ruined since the end of the eighteenth century.

## Haven

On the rocks underlying the north cliff of the promontory on which the castle stands are a series of post-holes and the remains of a breakwater, all that is left of the Haven referred to in a document of the year 1565, when the Earl of Morton was designated 'Keeper of the Haven of Thomptalloun'.

## Crane-Bastion

The ruin of a CRANE-BASTION overlooking the bay and the ox-road is to be seen on the cliff top 183 m south-south-east of the Outer Gate.

The freestone used for the castle was quarried at Canty Bay and also at the bay to the north of the castle. At this point the cliff is known as 'The Gin Head', so named after the appliance used here for raising the stone. The face-work of Tantallon, especially of the curtain walls, makes an interesting study. The variety is due to individual styles of rubble building introduced by the masons employed. At the close of the nineteenth century Sir Walter Hamilton Dalrymple did much to save the castle from decay and since the guardianship of the building was taken over in 1924 by the Commissioners of H.M. Works, the whole fabric has been thoroughly overhauled and the outworks reduced by excavation to their original level. During the operations a number of large stone shot, iron cannon balls, bombs, and lead shot of unusual character were unearthed. Among other relics found were medieval keys of iron, buckles, tags, mountings and chains of brass, foreign jettons [mostly of Nuremberg origin], Scottish coins and fragments of pottery of fifteenth- and sixteenth-century date. Some of the ware represented indicates an importation from Germany and the Low Countries. A selection of these articles is in the National Museum of Antiquities, Queen Street, Edinburgh, while others remain at Tantallon.

# HISTORY

'Dentaloune', a castellated site, appears on a map which has been dated as before 1300. Any evidence of an early fort, if such existed where Tantallon now stands, has long since disappeared, traces remaining only in the Celtic origin of the name. At the beginning of the fourteenth century it was in the possession of the Earls of Fife who held the lands in the vicinity and had founded a convent for Cistercian nuns at North Berwick.

## Earls of Douglas

It is in connection with the great House of Douglas that the castle is renowned in Scottish history. There is no clear evidence as to how or when this family entered into possession but in 1374 William, first Earl of Douglas and Mar, writes from 'our Castle of Temptaloun', and it is not improbable that by favour of King Robert II he became Castellan of Tantallon after the Earldom of Fife passed into the hands of Robert, Earl of Menteith, and the lands and castle may have been held as a tenancy from Isabella, Countess of Fife.

Before the year 1357 the Earl of Douglas married Margaret, sister of Thomas, Earl of Mar. Later, he made his brother-in-law's widow, who had assumed the style of Countess of Angus and Mar, his mistress, and she took up her residence at Tantallon. After the death of her nephew, the second Earl of Douglas, at Otterburn, Robert, Earl of Menteith, visiting the castle as Superior in February 1388, found her 'suiornand' [sojourning] there and granted her permission to remain, as witnessed by the following interesting document:

> 'Be yt chnawyn til al men throch this presens us Robert Steward, Eril of Fyff and of Myntheth, hat freely grantyt wil wr fufd cosyn dame Margaret Steward, Countess of Marr & Angus, the qwilk we fand suiornand in the Castel of Temtaloun, and qwilk we hadd now in ward, so sal necht be removyt out toff na Innys na ezis that so had befor or we come thair, bot ethr we sal ekyr na payrt in all gudnes and als lang as hir likys that to duel, so sal be ondistrenyt throch we, or ony that sal enter that Castel, throch we to do ony thing in the contrar of hir awyn wil, and qwhen that hir likys to remofe, so sal haf, fre issor and lief to pass at hir wil and hir mene, hir famyl, with al thair gudye, wyth outyn ony impediment in thair passage: And, in the men tyme, we haf left treuly we sal manteyn hir, hir men, hir landys and al hir possessons aganys

ony that wald warng thaim, in als tendir maner as wr awyn propir: In the wytnes of this thingis, wr soil is put to this presans. Gyfyn at Temptaloun, this tuenty day of Fauvare, the yeir of wr Lord a thusand thre hondir achty and acht.'

On the death of the second Earl of Douglas and Mar the castle and lands were claimed by the Earl of Fife who, in accordance with feudal custom, ought to have gone in person to receive them. As an excuse for not performing this duty he pleaded the cares of State and on his application the King wrote to the freeholders and inhabitants of the Barony of North Berwick and to Alan Lauder, Keeper and Constable of Tantallon, directing them to obey the Earl of Fife in all things and to render up the fortress to him.

## George Douglas, 1st Earl of Angus

Whatever may have been the Countess of Angus's moral delinquency, her astuteness ensured her domicile in the castle for she established her son George Douglas, whose father was her brother-in-law, in an honourable position by resigning in his favour the Earldom of Angus and doubtless brought about his marriage to Mary, second daughter of King Robert II. This George was the first Earl of Angus of the Douglas line. He was captured by the English at the battle of Homildon and died in 1403 of plague contracted during his captivity. His son William, the second Earl, was among the Scottish nobles who in April 1424, met King James I at Durham after his long exile and escorted him into his own realm. In 1425 he was one of the lords who, under the presidency of the King, condemned to the scaffold Murdoch, Duke of Albany, his two sons and the aged Earl of Lennox, and was responsible for the warding of the widowed Duchess of Albany [Countess of Fife] in Tantallon. While there the Duchess received from the Lord High Treasurer an allowance for dress and adornment. Four years later Alastair, Lord of the Isles, was imprisoned there after he had done a humiliating penance at Holyrood, 'dressed only in his shirt and drawers', unless the national costume of the Gael was mistaken for these garments.

James, who succeeded his father as third Earl, wielded great feudal authority and made Tantallon his headquarters. He withdrew thither in 1443 and was joined by Crichton in resisting the royal forces. A raid upon Strabrock and Abercorn, the lands of Earl William, Chieftain of the Black Douglases, resulted in a destructive incursion by the latter's forces under Fleming of Biggar, upon the lands of Angus in the vicinity of the castle. Fleming was captured and imprisoned in Tantallon. Angus, being in rebellion, was summoned before Parliament but preferred to remain at Tantallon. In

13

January 1446 decree of forfeiture was pronounced against him. A few months later Angus died.

In 1452 James II granted the castle and lands to George, a brother of the late Earl, who had succeeded to the title and had been appointed Warden of the Marches. In the Black Douglas Rebellion of 1455 this Red Douglas received a high command in the King's army, and having completely routed the rebels at Arkinholm [Langholm] on 18 May of that year, was rewarded with the Lordship of Douglas. In August 1460 he was present at the siege of Roxburgh Castle, and the cannon 'quhilk brak in the fyring' killed the King and slightly wounded the Earl. Seven days later at Kelso, Angus was well enough to place the crown on the boy King's head, exclaiming as he did so, 'There! Now that I have set it upon your Grace's head, let me see who will be so bold as to move it.'

## Archibald, 5th Earl of Angus ('Bell-the-Cat')

On the death of Earl George, in 1463, his son Archibald succeeded as fifth Earl. He is better known in Scottish history by the nickname of 'Bell-the-Cat', which he earned through his high-handed action at Lauder in 1482. The further efforts of Bell-the-Cat were quite in accordance with the times. He entered into a treasonable contract with the King of England, in consequence of which King James IV, on 25 July 1491, ordered Angus, who was than at Perth, to ward himself in Tantallon. The Earl defied the Royal authority, hastened to his stronghold and made speedy preparations to defend it.

## Tantallon besieged by King James IV October 1491

On 11 October the King laid siege to Tantallon; he sent 'Quarioir the gunnar' to Edinburgh 'to help furth with the gunnes' which were hastily collected from there and from Linlithgow. Crossbows and culverins were brought from Leith, and on the 13th workmen were cutting trenches. Seamen were dispatched in a boat to Largo to bring the King's ship, *The Flower*, which no doubt was utilised to blockade the castle from the sea. During the siege the King spent some of his leisure moments playing cards, as indicated by the Lord High Treasurer's Accounts, which record the King's loss of 'XVIII unicorns and II French crowns'.

Bell-the-Cat must have patched up his quarrel with the King for the latter sent him at Christmas, as a gift, 'a black velvet gown lined with lambs wool and with bukram to the tail of it'. Angus then seemed to have the confidence of his sovereign as, in 1492, he became Chancellor of Scotland; but later, again falling into disgrace, he was warded for some months in Dumbarton Castle.

The campaign which ended so disastrously for Scotland on Flodden Field was Bell-the-Cat's last appearance on the stage of Scottish history; as he was advanced in years he was probably not with the invading army but his two sons, George, Master of Angus, and Sir William of Glenbervie, were among the flower of Scottish chivalry who, along with Scotland's King, were struck down on that fateful field.

## Bishop Gavin Douglas

Gavin Douglas, the Earl's third son, and later Bishop of Dunkeld, studied at St Andrews University and became Rector of Prestonkirk and Priest of East Linton, a charge which brought him to the vicinity of his father's castle. Although he was a power in the state Gavin Douglas is best remembered for his poetic works; of his extant poems the best known are *The Palace of Honour*, *King Hart* and his *Translation of the Æneid of Virgil*.

John Major, or Mair, another eminent man of letters of this period, was born at the small township of Gleghornie, about 3 km south of Tantallon.

## Archibald, 6th Earl of Angus, and Queen Margaret Tudor

Archibald, the sixth Earl, son of the Master of Angus who was killed at Flodden, succeeded his grandfather, Bell-the-Cat. His first wife having died, he married in 1514 Queen Margaret, widow of King James IV, and was a figurehead in the many enterprises of violence, treason and corruption which rent and maimed the stability of the Kingdom. Angus and the Queen Mother entered into treasonable negotiations with her brother King Henry VIII and Cardinal Wolsey for the removal of the infant King and his brother to the English court. The Queen went to England in 1516, and her 'jowellis and baggis' were sent to her from Tantallon in September of that year. An inventory of these possessions is included in the Register of the Privy Council.

In 1515 John, Duke of Albany, became Regent and guardian of the Royal children. He straightway showed a strong hand, proclaimed Angus a traitor and seized Tantallon. In the following year the castle was returned to Angus. In an agreement dated 28 March 1516, between the Commissioners appointed by the Regent and the Earl, the following interesting passage occurs: 'and gif his charter kyst be broken in Temptalloun and his evidentis takin furth thar of sa mony as he wantis, till gif him of new'. Angus probably had reason to complain. On the next occasion when Parliament decreed forfeiture against him in 1528, he secretly transferred the muniments from the charter chest to a large beef-pot, had the lid securely clasped with iron, and the pot buried under a little bridge near the farthest gate of the castle. The legs of the pot stood upon the solid rock, preserving the contents from water, and there the charters remained undamaged until recovered by the Earl on his return from exile in England fifteen years later.

In 1517 Angus was appointed one of the six Regents. This resulted in a quarrel with his wife which, however, was patched up later, the Queen being escorted into Edinburgh by Angus with four hundred horsemen. Welcomed by the citizens with 'shooting of guns and great melody of instruments playing', their arrival unfortunately was followed by the episode known as 'Cleanse the Causeway', a fray conducted in the High Street of Edinburgh. The Earl and his supporters there defeated Arran, Archbishop Beaton, and the rest of the Albany adherents. Albany returned from France in November 1521 and forced Angus, who had again quarrelled with his wife, to go into exile in that country. Returning through England in 1524, Angus took up his abode at Tantallon, whence he communicated with King Henry concerning the Queen's ambassadors and desiring money. In 1525, much to the gratification of King Henry VIII, Angus was appointed warden of the East and Middle Marches; again falling into disfavour he was relieved of the wardenship and ordered by King James to 'pass and remain north of the Spey'. Angus, however, preferred to entrench himself behind his own strong walls of Tantallon and to wait the coming storm. Here he was joined by his brother Sir George and by his kinsman, Sir Archibald Douglas of Kilspindie. This action was followed by an Act of Parliament which decreed forfeiture of their lives, lands and goods. The day on which the sentence was promulgated, the Earl with the permission of the warden of the English Marches, slipped over the Border where he awaited an opportunity to return. Tantallon was seized by the King, who determined to hold it in his own hands, but during harvest time he found it necessary to dismiss his army. This was the Earl's opportunity; he came back to his castle to make hasty preparations against a siege before withdrawing once more to the vicinity of the Border.

A summons to arms was issued on 7 September 1528 in the King's name and in the following terms:

'Attour ordanis lettres be direct to all the schereffis of Scotland and thar deputis chargeand all and sindry lordis, barouns, fre haldaris, gentilmen landit and uthiris substancius gentilmen within the boundis of thar offices als wele to

PLATE I    Tantallon Castle from the air with Bass Rock beyond

PLATE 2   The castle from the west . . .

PLATE 3   . . . and from the south

PLATE 4   A general view of the curtain wall and Mid Tower from the south west

PLATE 5   The curtain wall and Mid Tower from the west. The forework, added
to the Mid Tower after 1529, can be clearly seen

PLATE 6   In the foreground is the Outer Gate, once arched and with a massive
double door, and flanked on the right by the gun-looped spur-work

PLATE 8    The Close, with the Sea Gate on the right

PLATE 9    The seaward end of the northern Courtyard Range showing the
           remains of the kitchen, bakehouse and stair foundation.
           The Bass Rock is in the background

PLATE 7    Tantallon—surrounded on three sides by the sea

burgh as to land, spirituale as temporale landis, that thai be in Edinburgh in thar best manere bodin for weir the XX day of Octobre nixt tocum furnist with provisioune and vitalis for XX dais nixt eftir that cuming to his grace, ilk persoune under the pane of tynsale of lif, landis and gudis to pas with the kingis [grace] for recovering of the house of Temptalloun furth of the handis of Archibald sumtym erle of Angus and uthiris his part takaris declarit tratouris and rebellis for certane poyntis of tresoun: and gif ony man labouris to gett ane licence to remain at hame nochtwithstanding the premissis, the samin sall nocht excus thame nor na licence gevin or to be gevin, bot sall incurr the saidis panys but ony favouris.'

Before the army could assemble, Patrick, Earl of Bothwell, Sheriff of Edinburgh and Haddington, undertook at the instance of the Privy Council to keep the rebels in check for ten days from 10 October, although he could not actually blockade the castle.

## Tantallon besieged by the King

On 23 October 1528, King James laid siege to Tantallon with cannon, some of which he borrowed from Dunbar Castle—'two great cannones throwen mouthed mow and her marrow, with two great boatcards and two moyanis, two double falkons and four quarter falkons with their powder and bullets and gunners for to use them'. While on the way to attack, according to an old legend, the King's soldiers beat on their drums a rhythm, 'Ding Doon Tantalloun, Ding Doon Tantalloun'. This is supposed to be the origin of the 'Scot's March'. Tantallon, however, was not to be 'ding doon'; the attackers could make no impression on the stronghold and after twenty days the King rasied the siege, whereat Angus immediately returned to his fortress and with one hundred and sixty adherents followed up and captured before the 'skreigh o' day' the slow-retreating train of artillery. This episode is recounted by Angus in his letter to the Earl of Northumberland, which reads as follows:

'My Lord, in my maist hertly manere I commend me unto zour gud lordschip and to certify the sammyn of six novelles as occuris here. Emplesit zour lordship, call to rememberance how the King my master assemblit his army the xxiii day of October last bipast, nochtwithstanding the tender and special lettrez the Kingis hienes of Eingland directit to his grace in favouris of me, and incontrar the said convocacioune of asseigeing of my houss of Temtalloune, at the quhilk he and his army, with artaillierie of his awin and of Dombar Castell in greit quantite has lyne and assiegit ryeht scharply baithe be gunnis and inginiouss menne, baithe Scottis and Frenche, that myndit the wallis in sic sort that as can be rememberit, thare was nevir sa mekill pane, travell, expensis, and diligence done and maid for the wynnyng of ane houss and the sammyn escaip in Scotland

17

sen it was first inhabit; and apone Weddynnsday, the ferde of November, the King removit to Edinbrurght, bot xvi mylis fra Temtalloune, and left ane band of fut menne and ane cumpany of horss menne to convoy hame the artillierie: and that sammyn Weddynnisday, at nycht I, and part of wele horssit menne of myn awin, to noumer of aucht score, and levit the lave of my folkis behynd me at Temtalloune, followit in efter thame, and a litill efter the mone rysing or it was day, set upon thame, and has defait thame all, loving to God, baithe horss menne end fut menne, and slane David Falconer, principall capitane of the fut menne, the best man of wer in Scotland on the sey, and was takin be Einglismenne nocht lang ago; and I have takin ane uther capitane of the fut menne, and has him in firmance; and also I tuk the maister of the artaillie, and wane all the sammyn, and had baithe menne and artaillierie all in my will and dangare; bot becauss the King my maister is sa neir of blud to the Kingis hienes of Eingland, that has done sa mekill for me, and sa gud and graciouss prince to me, and mekill the better be zour solicitacioune; I wald nocht dishonour the King here sa fer as to hald his artaillie bot convoyit the sammyn my selff quhill it was furthe of danger and sufferit the maister of artaillie to pas, and prayit him to commend my lauly service unto my soverane, and to schew his grace that I have bene trew servand and subject to the sammyn, and that I gave his grace na wyte of ocht that was done to me, bot to the evill avisit personis about his grace nocht worthy thereto, and had done sich dishonour to him at this tyme thai mycht nevir amend it, and I had plesit put it to executioune, My Lord, thir premissis ar of verite, and howbeit I mycht have ane way and appointment, I will do na thing therein bot be the ordinance of the Kingis hienes of Eingland and the aviss of zour lordschip, and hes writtin presently to the Kingis hienes to send command to the Commissionaris nocht to tac na trewis nor paex without I and my frendis be restorit to our heritagis, benefices, offices, rumys and possessiouns, and his grace abyding thereat, I knaw perfit all wilbe as his hienes will have it. And forther, in every behalff my brother zour servand cann informe zour lordschip, quhame God conserve eternaly, written at Coldinghame Abbay this Setterday.

Yours

Ard, Erl off Anguss.

To my Lord Erle of Northeumbreland,
lieutennent and wardane generall of the Merchis of Eingland,
foranentis Scotland.'

On 26 January 1529 Patrick, Earl of Bothwell, was again invited to take command of operations at Tantallon for the expulsion of Archibald and George Douglas, 'for the space of ane yer and ferthir endurand the Kingis will . . . and the Kingis grace to furnis artalzery and munitions.

'For the quhilkis causis the said erle Bothwell sall have the lands of Temptallon in few farme and heritage payand yerly tharfor IC merkis of few alanerlie'.

Angus had attempted to seek a reconciliation with the King, offering to surrender all his castles and to do loyal service in future as he had done in the past. James, with the consent of his Council, accepted the offer provided Tantallon was given up to him at once.

## Tantallon in Crown Hands

To this Angus would not agree and continued to reside there in security, supporting himself by raids on the adjoining countryside until the middle of May 1529, when he retired into exile in England, and the castle was surrendered to the King, who furnished it with men and guns and appointed Oliver Sinclair captain of the castle. For the next fourteen years Tantallon was in Crown hands and considerable works of repair and consolidation were made in order to strengthen it against the forces of improved artillery. The King, according to the historian Lindsay of Pitscottie, 'causit maissounis cum and rainforce samin wallis quhilk was left waist of befoir as transses and throw passagis and maid all massie work to that effect that it sould be unwinabill in tymes comming to ony enemies that would come to persew it'.

In 1535 Sir John Ersking was granted an annuity for keeping and fortifying the castle and entries in the Master of Works' accounts for the years 1537–39 show that works were in progress at the time under John Skrimgeour of Myres, King's Master of Works, the master mason being George Sempill.

On the death of the King after the battle of Solway Moss, 24 November 1542, Angus returned from exile and was restored to his estates. Assisted by his brother, Sir George, he continued to keep up a treasonable connection with Henry VIII, from whom he had received a pension while in England.

Henry wrote to his principal agent, Sir Ralph Sadler, the English Ambassador, on 2 September 1543, that he desired Tantallon or Dunbar Castle as a place in which to keep his 'treasour' the moneys that were to be paid out in bribes to ruin the Realm of Scotland.

The countries were now at war and Sadler applied to Angus for permission to live at Tantallon. On 25 October he wrote from Edinburgh—'and thought as I coulde perceyve thErle of Anguisshe had no greate good will to lett me lye in his house of Temptallon, bicause the same be unfurnisshed and almoste all the lodginges taken downe to be newe buyldyd. Yet at the last rather than take me with theim westwards, he was contente to lende me Temptallon, but he said I myght not remove thider till within fyve or six deayes aftre there departure out of this towne for the house coulde no sooner be readye for me ... But I sent a servaunte of myne owne to Temptallon, who brought me wourde that the house was clearly unfurnisshed bothe of beddinge and all manner of householde stuff, and none to be brought nor hyred.' Sadler was living in Tantallon by 6 November, for he wrote on that day, 'Wherfore I am desired to remayne here in Temptallon, which though it be but easyly furnished and sclender lodginge in it, yet I assure you it is of suche strenght as I nede not to feare the malice of myne enymeys and therefore do thinke myself nowe to be out of daungier.'

On 16 November, James, Earl of Arran, wrote a letter of remonstrance to Angus, pointing out that he had had delivered to Sadler at Tantallon orders for him to leave the country. Sadler, however, had refused; 'and he nochwithstanding the samyn remainis still practisand privatlie amangis oure soverane ladeis lieges, corrumpand, be money and uther syndrie ways, grete menn of the realme to the evident supplanting and undermyneing of this cunitrey and faithfull subgettis thairof'. Finally Arran requested Angus 'to caus the said imbassatour depart out of zour said hous of Temptalloune'. Sadler took up the role of 'Willie Wastle', not only defied the Regent but refused to leave, and wrote to Suffolk for help, stating that 'The Governor' [Arran] 'will besiege this house of Temptallon, which is strong ynough to abyde his siege, and metely well furnisshed with artillery, but it is veray sclenderly furnisshed with vitaile, specially of wheate and malte, and also of cole, so that if we be besieged, oneles your lordships will helpe to furnisshe us out of Englonde by see, which maye be done mawgre all Scotland,—we shall bothe lacke fyer and also be famysshed.'

Sadler was evidently acting on King Henry's instructions to hold the castle, as the latter wrote to Suffolk stating: 'Wherfor youe shall say unto the sayd Sir George [Douglas], that in cace he be unprovided of men and municion for the defence of the sayd castle of Tyntallon, we wil be contented to appoynt a trusty man of ours with a sufficient granison to take charge for the savegarde of the same, and wil with diligence if nede be, se it furnished by see of artillery and all other kynd of municion for defence of the same accordingly.' A postscript adds: 'In cace that thErle of Anguish or Sir George fearyng the soubdayn surprise of the castle of Tyntallon, and beyng not able to furnish it with men and municioun sufficient, shall offre the same into our tuicion, and be contented we lay a garnison there of our (men) for the defence thereof, our pleasure is youe shall provide shippes with a garnison of men artillery and municion at Newcastle, convenient for the furniture of the sayd castle, and to send the same thither under sum gentleman a servaunt of ours and beyng a man of stomak . . . [to be] Capitayn and to take gard of the sayd castle and to receyve therwith the sayd garnison and furniture of municion, without redyliveryng or surrendryng the same to any person until he shall know our pleasure in that behalf.' Suffok in his reply, dated 15 November, informs the King, 'And wher your majeste writeth to have Temptallon to be made sure for surprisings, and to be furnisshed with vitaile and ordinaunce accordingly: I asked of Sir George at his beinge here with me bicause of Mr. Sadleyrs lettres, howe it was furnisshed? Who said to me there was no feare in it, for as he thought it was furnisshed well, and all the substaunce that his brodyr and he and all theyr frendes had, was in it, and that they had ordinaunce that wolde shote two mylys and ynough of it. Wherein he said he wolde write to his brodyr to se to it surely to be furnisshed furthwith; at which tyme I tolde him that if he lacked ought, I shulde helpe to se him furnisshed.'

On 9 December, King Henry's Privy Council communicated the news to Suffolk that 'his majeste entendeth to sende shortely unto youe his servant Rogers to be conveyed to Temptallon to viewe the castle secretely and to bring his majeste a true plat and perfaict description of every parte of the same'. It seems highly probable that this was never accomplished for Angus was again subject to a remonstrance from the Regent Arran and on 12 December Sadler writes from Berwick to say that 'Mr Douglas cam yesterdaye to me with en honest conpanye of gentilmen and their traynes to the nombre of fowre hundreth horse or there aboutes, and hathe verie freendlie this daye broughte me hither in safetie'.

In April 1544 the Master of Morton, Angus's son, held Tantallon at Henry's pleasure and an attempt to victual it by boat from Aberdour was frustrated. In that year John Douglas and Alexander Jardine were keepers. On 6 April, Hertford informed King Henry that 'The said priest [Sir John Penvan, King Henry VIII's chaplain] tolde us also that he had sent this message unto the capteyn of Temptallen that for as moche as thErill of Anguishe was nowe in warde in Hamylton castell, he should therefore loke to his charge, and kepe surely the said castell of Temptallen, and not to delyver the same to the Governour nor no Skotishman, notwithstanding that theEril shulde sende any wryting, comaundment or token for the delyvere thereof, unles the said erle came thither him silf in persone. And if he wolde delyver the same into your majestes handes or to suche as your highnes shulde appoynt to receyve yt to your use, the said priest saith he promysed him gert reward and enterteignement for him silf and all the gonners and souldiors that were in yt, so that they shuld be made men whyles they lyved, and also offered that he that shuld receyve yt to your highnes use, shulde be bounde to delyver yt agayne to thEril of Anguishe when he shalbe at libertie, if then he shall requyre the same.

'the said priest tolde me thEril of Hertforde, that commonyng lately with the said Erle of Anguishe for the delyvere of hostages to your majeste for the performance of suche thinges as shuld be nowe pacted at Carlisle, the said erle said that he knewe not whome he shuld ley for hostage, and the priest answered that he might well delyver Temptallon to your highness for hostage. Whereunto thEril replyed, that if your majeste came with your armye into Scotland, he wolde delyver yt to your highnes if every stone were of golde. And the priest asked him agayne, whether he wold not likewise delyver yt to your lieutenant? Whereunto the said erle answered that in that sorte he wolde be well advised or be delyvered yt.'

In 1543 Angus was still receiving liberal bribes from Henry to promote the English projects. His treasonable correspondence with the latter having fallen into the hands of Cardinal Beaton's party, Angus and his brother Sir George were seized and imprisoned in Blackness Castle in 1544. Sir George's sons, David and James, had actually offered to surrender Tantallon to the invaders. It would assuredly have been ill for the two prisoners had not the English fleet under Hertford arrived in the Forth at an opportune moment and effected their rescue. Tantallon lay near the line of march of the invading English army yet it was not attacked by Hertford, he being 'constrayned to leave yt for lack of carriages for gret peces of artillerye and also for lack of powder'.

Hertford seized Leith and marched to Edinburgh but owing to the resistance put up by the inhabitants and by the guns of the castle, the English had to content themselves with the burning of Holyrood: but they harried Scotland as far as Stirling and thence to the Borders. At Melrose the tombs of the Douglases were desecrated, an action which resulted in Angus associating himself with the national cause. He was appointed Lieutenant of Southern Scotland but resigned this command in 1545 when he once more solicited to help Henry who, however, having had enough of him, replied by offering two thousand crowns for the Earl's head. The death of the English king did not stop further incursions but it gave Angus an opportunity of proving himself true to the Auld Kingdom. At Pinkie Cleuch, fought and lost on 10 September 1547, Angus, though somewhat reluctant, commanded the advance guard. Ten days thereafter we find Sir George writing from Tantallon asking favour from Hertford for himself and his own friends and requesting the latter not to destroy their lands in the Borders.

## 1548. French Galley sunk off Tantallon

On 4 August 1548 a French galley was sunk by the English in a naval encounter off Tantallon, and 'the gunnarres of Temptalloun that war schutand at the Inglishe schippis' were awarded drink silver to the amount of fourteen shillings, Scots; in May 1554 the gunners and the porter were given £5, 4s. Scots in drink silver on the occasion of the widowed Queen's visit to the castle.

Angus died at Tantallon in January 1556–57, and was succeeded by his nephew, David, who died a few months afterwards; it is doubtful whether the latter ever took up the title, or was feudally vested in the estates. On 3 February, immediately after the sixth Earl's death, on the authority of the Queen the castle was handed over to the keeping of the Laird of Craigmillar and a schedule of the munition and artillery equipment of the castle was made. This document, a copy of which is appended, is preserved in H.M. Register House, Edinburgh.

In June 1558 repairs were carried out by the Crown; the timber for the building was despatched in John Dalmahoy's boats from Leith and in September six barrowmen were employed for ten days in cleaning the draw-well for which a great tow was provided.

David's son, Archibald, succeeded as the eighth Earl, being then not more than two years old. At that time the stronghold was in the keeping of George Drummond of Blair on behalf of the Crown. Drummond had a small garrison of seven horsemen and twenty-two footmen. As he was put to considerable expense while Captain of the Castle, the Crown reimbursed him on 23 January to the extent of £610 Scots. In 1562 John Learmonth was captain, but in 1565–66 the Earl's uncle and tutor, James, Earl of Morton, took the castle over under an obligation that it should be 'reddie and patent to her Majestie' so long as it was in his hands. In March, however, Mary Queen of Scots ordered the castle to be handed over to 'the lordis of the Bas elder and younger' and an inventory of the munition in the castle to be furnished. She visited Tantallon in November 1566.

When the young Earl was eighteen he demanded from his uncle, the Regent, the great brass pot of Tantallon in which the sixth Earl had buried his charters on going into exile and which had been taken away by Morton. The latter's reply was, 'I have had more broth to put in it than that it should stand empty at Tantallon'. Angus was appointed Warden of the West Marches in June 1577 and a year later Lieutenant-General of the Realm. When Esme Stuart, Duke of Lennox, and James Stuart, Earl of Arran, directed the proceedings against Morton, which ultimately sealed the latter's doom, Angus removed all his valuables from Dalkeith and Aberdour to the stronger fortalice of Tantallon and entered into treasonable negotiations with Queen Elizabeth's ambassador, Thomas Randolph.

## 1577. Angus in Exile in England

Angus was proclaimed a traitor and five days after Morton's execution in June sentence of forfeiture and outlawry was passed upon him.

He immediately went into exile in England and was received at the court of Elizabeth where, according to Godscroft, the historian who accompanied him, the Earl became intimate with Sir Philip Sidney. The latter had just finished writing his *Arcadia* and delighted to entertain the Scottish nobleman by reading it aloud to him.

In 1581 the Castle was in Crown hands, King James VI authorising William, Lord Ruthven, the owner of Dirleton Castle, to supply for 'the sustentation of the kepairs of the Castle of Thomptalloun samekle daylie to the kepairs thairof as Andro Hume had the tyme that he kepit the samin'. Angus was permitted to return to Scotland in September 1582. Shortly afterwards, however, the King was informed that the Earl was fortifying Tantallon, 'but at the end it was known to the King that he kept his house quietly and that he repaired the shackles of an old brewhouse without any other fortifications'. The Earl's opposition to the Arran faction caused his banishment north of the Spey, and finally further exile in England when the Earl took with him his valuables and various domestic fabrics which he handed over to the safe-keeping of Lord Hunsdon, Governor of Berwick. An inventory of these goods exists.

## 1585. Return of Angus

On 6 April 1584, Angus, then 'Keeper of the Castle of Thomptalloun', was commanded to deliver the castle to the King's officers and ten days later it is recorded as being held for the Crown by the Earl of Rothes. The Earl's estate and dignities were, however, restored on 4 November 1585. In the Register of the Privy Council, Alexander Douglas is given as 'Captain of Temptalloun'.

Angus died without male issue on 4 August 1588, aged thirty-four, of a disease attributed to an evil spell cast by one Agnes Sampson, who was condemned as a witch and expiated the crime on the Castle Hill of Edinburgh, 'thair bund to ane staik and wirrett quhill sche was deid, and thairefter hir body to be brunt in assis'.

The Earldom then reverted to William Douglas of Glenbervie, grandson of Bell-the-Cat's second son, Sir William Douglas of Braidwood. This Earl was a staunch Protestant but his eldest son, William, who succeeded him as tenth Earl on his death in July 1591, was a Roman Catholic who for his faith had suffered exile in 1589; the following year, however, he embraced the Protestant religion and was restored to favour. Proving a lukewarm adherent he reverted after three years to Papistry. Because of this the General Assembly took active proceedings against him and in 1608 he was ordered to ward himself in Glasgow. On 25 May, Angus wrote to the King, 'that giff I salbe wairdit, it may ather be in Thomptalloun, Edinburgh or

Leithe quhair I may have the help and assistance of phisitianis for my secknes that in Glasgow quhilk is ane place verie vruneit for one for sundrie respectis but speciallie for recoverie of my hethe'. The King lent a deaf ear to William's prayer, so he was confined at Glasgow and subjected to perpetual examination and rebuke by the representatives of the Presbytery of that city and the Synod of Clydesdale, who could make no headway against the recalcitrant Earl and reported to the Assembly that he was 'obstinat and abderat in heresie of papestre'. On 21 September he was excommunicated according to the order of the King and after a short term of close imprisonment was allowed to go into voluntary exile in France because of his 'present grite inhabilitie and seiknes of whiche he has no grite hope evir to recover without the help and advise of physitionis in foreyne partis'. In his testament dated 31 October 1608, among other details, he ordained that 'mionitioun wapinis and airmour within the Castle of Thomptalloun remain within the said Castle'. Stephen Bruntfield was Captain of Tantallon in 1597.

## Cromwell

The Earl died in France in March 1611 and was buried at Paris in the Abbey Church of Saint Germain-des-Pres. His son, William, succeeded him as eleventh Earl, and was created Marquess of Douglas. In 1639 Tantallon was yielded to the Covenanters being defended by only a few of the Earl's retainers while he was attending the General Assembly and the Committee of Estates. Towards the close of 1650 a body of thirty horse, 'desperado gallants', had established themselves within the stronghold. Their attacks on Cromwell's lines of communication were so thorough and well planned that it was reported to the Protector that 'they had taken more men and done us more harm than the whole Scots army and all their other garrisons'. This resulted in the place being attacked by General Monk with 2000–3000 men about February 1651, when, after burning the hamlet of Castleton and driving the defenders into Tantallon, he captured it after a twelve-day bombardment with a battery of granadoes and six battering pieces. It is said that the garrison first beat a parley, then hung out a 'little clout', finally a great sheet, all of which tokens of surrender were disregarded. At last the Governor himself had to come out upon the wall to request a parley; this was granted and the garrison then marched out, 'about fourscore men, and about a dozen good horses'. Another account says 91 officers and soldiers; within the Castle were 15 or 16 great guns and about 120 spare arms'. The narrative of Sir James Balfour, however, gives the following description:

'Fryday, 21 Febrij, 1651. About 4 in the eiuning Tantallon Castle, in Louth-ean, was randred to Cromwell, after he had battred at the wall for 12 dayes continually with grate canon. Capitane Alexander Setton defendit the same gallantly; bot after that the enimeyes canon had oppind a werey large breache, and filled the dray ditche with the wall, he entered it by storme. The Capitane and thesse few men (which) were with him, betooke themselves to (the) tower, and resolued to sell ther lives at als good a rait as they could, if that quarter should (be) denayed them; bot the enimey seinng them stand gallantly to it, preferrid them quarters, which they excepted.'

The capture of Tantallon brought the release of a number of English prisoners, including seamen, from a ship captured by the Captain of the Bass on 11 January. It is probable that a small garrison of the Protector's forces was provided as General Monk, writing from Dalkeith on 15 October 1657, regarding the proposed disposition of troops in Scotland noted, 'Tymptallon and the Bass one company of 35'. The Earl of Angus was in residence shortly after Monk's attack but the castle had made its last appearance as a military factor and never again was considered a fortress.

In a 1670 inventory mention is made of the following, 'the drawling', 'four iron yetts at the entrie', 'an iron yett at the tumbler' (trap door?) and a wooden portcullis shod with iron. The following places within the building are specified—'the welchamber', 'the garden chamber', 'the dyneing roume', 'my ladies chamber', 'the lang hall', the chamber in the Douglas Tower, 'the reid' and 'the blew' chambers and the 'lang loft'.

## 1699. Sir Hew Dalrymple purchases Tantallon

In 1699 the castle and barony were purchased from the Marquess of Douglas by Sir Hew Dalrymple, Lord President of the Court of Session, after which the structure was allowed to fall into decay and was used as a quarry for material to build the adjacent farm building and dykes.

# APPENDIX

## Inventory of Munition and Artillery, 1556

The mvnition and artaillerie being in the house and castell of Thomtalloun the tyme of the delyvuering of the samin be my lord of Cassillis thesaurar to our souerane ladie to the laird of Craigmyllar in the quenis grace name The thrid day of Feburiar The yeir of God etc., fifty sex yeir.

Within the said castell laich in the cloiss.

Ane culvering bastard of font.

Two singill slangis of Irne with two chalmeris to ather of thame.

Ane uther culvering bastard of font.

Ane heidsteik of Irne with tua chalmeris.

On the eist tourheid.

Ane culvering myoun with hir furnist stok and quhelis.

On the foir tour heid.

Ane culvering myoun with hir stockkis and quhelis.

Ane singill falcoun of font.

On Douglass tourheid.

Twa singill falconis of font.

Twa slangis of Irne without stokkis and with twa chalmeris to ather of thame.

Abone the brig.

Twa singill cutthrottis and ane dowbill cutthrott with twa chalmeris to ilk ane of thame.

In the werkhous.

Twa dowbill slangis with twa chalmeris to ather of thame.

Twa singill slangis with twa chalmeris to ather of thame.

Ane singill cutthrott with twa chalmeris.

In the entries of the zet.

Ane singill cutthrott with twa chalmeris.

At the zet.

Twenty twa pikkis.

Twelf halbertis.

In the mid tower.

Twelf pikkis.
    In the munition houss.
Twenty foir half haggis with yair stokkis.
Ten culverings with their stokkis and ane culvering without ane stok.
Four paris of cawmis of brass.
Aucht kynkynnis of powder with half ane barrall and ane quarter barrell of grof powder.
Ane half barrell brokin up of culvering powder half full or therby.
Fourtene powder hornis for culverings and half haggis.
XXII Luntis of the samin.
    In ane chalmer besyd the munition houss.
Sewin singill hagbuttis of font.
    In the hall loft.
Twa barrellis of powder.
    In ane volt vnder the hall.
Twa griet barrellis of powder.
Twa half barrellis of powder.
Ane hagbut of font without ane stok.
    In ane cellar under the hall.
Twa serpentynis stokkit with tre.
Within the said castell and place in sindrie partis thereof.
Certane bullettis of Irne to the estimatioun of twa hundredth or thereby.

NOTE. A culverin bastard was the smallest size of this type of gun; the bore was 10·2 cm (4 in.) and the shot about 3·2 kilos (7 lb.)
    A culverin moyen was a culverin of medium size, afterwards called a demiculverin; bore 11·4 cm (4½ in.) and shot about 4·5 kilos (10 lb.)
    An ordinary culverin was from 3 to 4 m (10 to 13 feet) long; the diameter of its bore from 12·7 to 14 cm (5 to 5½ in.) and the weight of shot from 7·7 kilos to 9 kilos (17 to 20 lb.)
    Cutthrottis were pieces of ordnance.
    Slangis, a kind of cannon resembling a culverin.
    Hagbut, a hand gun of the period.
    Half haggis were hagbuts of a small size, or arquebuses.

# GLOSSARY

| | |
|---|---|
| BARBICAN | An outward extension of a gateway |
| CHASE | Groove |
| CORBEL | A projection from a wall intended to support a weight |
| GARDEROBE | Latrine |
| GLACIS | A broad smoothly graded strip of ground sloping away from the wall of the Castle |
| IMPOST | The moulded or decorated stone at the springing of an arch |
| JAMBS | The sides of an opening |
| MACHICOLATION | An opening between corbels of a parapet or in a floor such as a vault of a gateway through which a garrison could assail besiegers with missiles |
| PORTCULLIS | An iron-shod wooden grille suspended by chains in grooves in front of a gate and let down to ground level in times of necessity |
| RAVELIN | In fortifications a detached triangular work with 2 faces meeting in a salient angle |
| REVETMENT | A retaining wall |
| TRAVERSE | A work to obstruct enfilading fire and attack |
| TRUNNION | Pivot for the drawbridge |
| TURN PIKE | A wheel stair: commonly a spiral stair |
| YETT | A gate (Scots) |

# Principal Authorities Quoted

*Calendar of documents relating to Scotland*, 1108–1509. Edited by JOSEPH BAIN, HM GENERAL REGISTER HOUSE, EDINBURGH.

*Calendar of Letters and Papers relating to the Affairs of the Borders of England and Scotland.* Edited by JOSEPH BAIN.

*The Exchequer Rolls of Scotland.* HM General Register House, Edinburgh.

*The Douglas Book*, by WILLIAM FRASER, CB.

*Letters and Papers illustrating the Political Relations of England and Scotland in the XVIth Century.* Edited by JOSEPH BAIN.

*A History of the House of Douglas*, by the Rt Hon Sir HERBERT MAXWELL, Bart. Edited by W A LINDSAY.

*Accounts of the Lord High Treasurer of Scotland*, 1473–1566. Edited by Sir JAMES BALFOUR PAUL.

Printed in Scotland by Her Majesty's Stationery Office at HMSO Press, Edinburgh
Dd 403118/2896 K200 4/80 (15183)

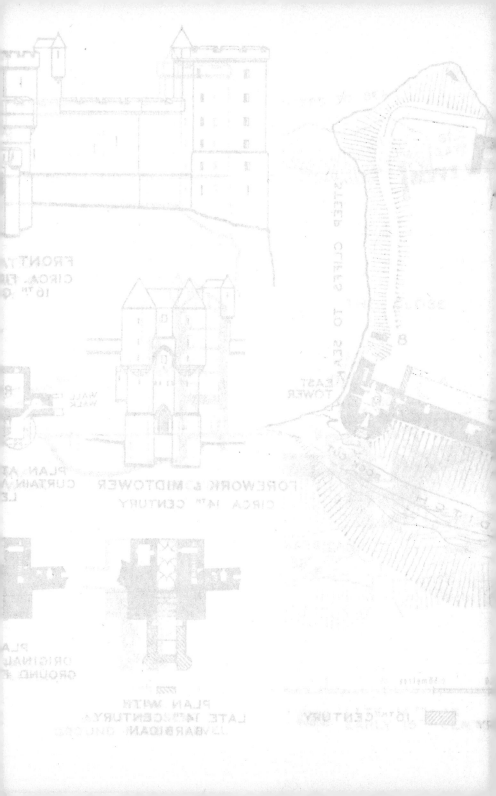

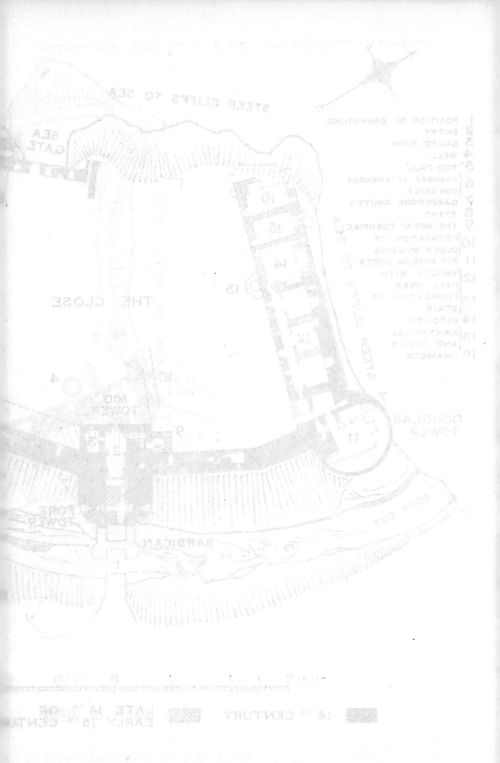

TANTALLON CASTLE